FAR

VOLUME ONE

All American Folk
Complete Sheet Music Editions

DISCARD

Catalog #07-1003

ISBN# 1-56922-040-9

Printed in the United States of America

Produced by John L. Haag

Exclusive Distributor:
CREATIVE CONCEPTS PUBLISHING CORPORATION
6020-B Nicolle Street, Ventura, California 93003
Check out our Web site at *http://www.creativeconcepts.com* or you can Email us at *mail@creativeconcepts.com*

CONTENTS

CONTENTS

Joan Baez

Buffy Sainte-Marie

Doc Watson

Lovin' Spoonful

Kingston Trio

The Brothers Four

Gordon Lightfoot

Chad Mitchell

Glenn Yarbrough

The New Christy Minstrels

Joni Mitchell

Janis Ian

Gale Garnett

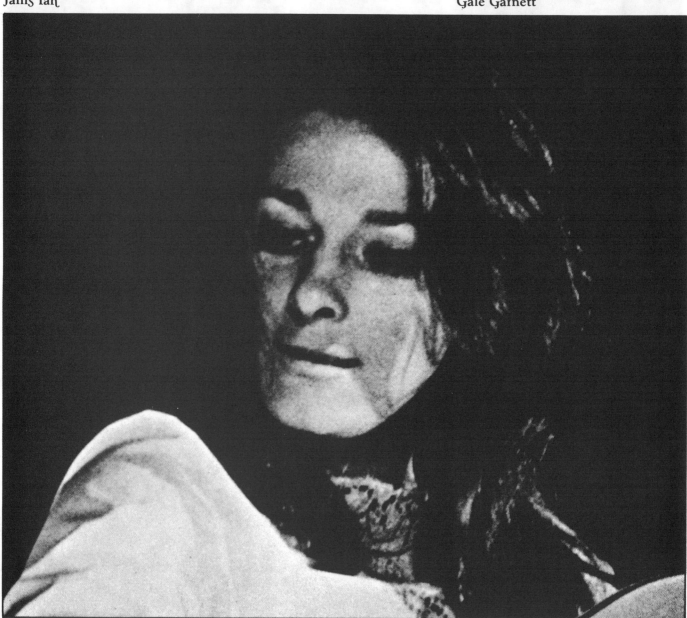

Judy Collins

Tim Rose

Peter, Paul & Mary

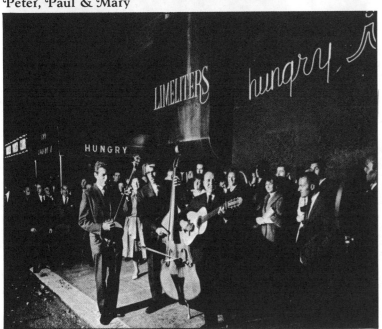

The Limelighters

Tim Harden

The Greenwood Singers

Carly Simon

Judy Henske

Seals & Croft

Ian and Sylvia

Hedy West

Woody Guthrie

John Stewart

Simon & Garfunkel

Village Stompers

The Byrds

Bob Dylan

John Denver

Donovan

Pete Seeger

Van Morrison

The Serendipity Singers

Richie Havens

Hoyt Axton

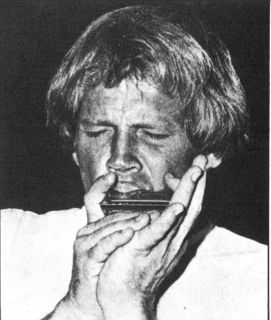

Barry Mc Guire

ALL MY TRIALS

Lyrics:

Hush, lit-tle ba-by, don't you cry, You know your Ma-ma was born to die.

The Riv-er Jor-dan is muddy and cold, It chills the bod-y, but not the soul.

If liv-ing were a thing money could buy, The rich would live and the poor would die.

All my tri-als, Lord. Soon be o-ver.

AMAZING GRACE

AMERICAN FOLK TRILOGY
Dixie/Battle Hymn Of The Republic/All My Trials

ARKANSAS TRAVELER

Medium Tempo

Oh, once up-on a time in Ar-kan-sas, An old man sat in his lit-tle cab-in door, And he

fid-dled at a tune that he liked to hear, A jol-ly old ___ tune that he played by ear. It was

rain - ing hard but the fid-dler did-n't care, He sawed a - way at the pop - u - lar air, Though his

roof - tree leaked like a wa - ter - fall, That did-n't seem to both - er the man at all.

A traveller was riding by that day,
And stopped to hear him a-fiddling away;
The cabin was afloat and his feet were wet,
But still the old man didn't seem to fret.
 So the stranger said, "Now the way it seems to me,
 You'd better mend your roof," said he.
 But the old man said as he played away:
 "I couldn't mend it now, it's a rainy day."

The traveller replied, "That's all quite true,
But this, I think is the thing for you to do;
Get busy on a day that is fair and bright,
Then patch the old roof till it's good and tight."
 But the old man kept on a-playing at his reel,
 And tapped the ground with his leathery heel.
 "Get along," said he, "for you give me a pain—
 My cabin never leaks when it doesn't rain!"

AURA LEE

Medium tempo

1. As the black-bird in the Spring, ___ 'Neath the wil-low tree, ___ Sat and piped, I
2. Take my heart and take my ring, I give my all to thee, ___ Take me for e-
3. In her blush the rose was born, 'Twas mu-sic when she spake, ___ In her eyes, the
4. AUR - A LEE, the bird may flee the wil-low's gold-en hair, ___ Then the win-try

heard him sing, In praise of AUR - A LEE. AU - RA LEE, AU - RA LEE,
ter - ni - ty, ___ dear-est AUR - A LEE. AU - RA LEE, AU - RA LEE,
light of morn, ___ spark-ling seemed to break. AU - RA LEE, AU - RA LEE,
winds may be ___ blow-ing ev-'ry-where, Yet if thy blue eyes I see,

Maid with gold - en hair, Sun-shine came a - long with thee, And swal-lows in the air. ___
Maid with gold - en hair, Sun-shine came a - long with thee, And swal-lows in the air. ___
Maid with gold - en hair, Sun-shine came a - long with thee, And swal-lows in the air. ___
Gloom will soon de - part, For to me, sweet AU - RA LEE Is sun-shine to the heart. ___

BAD GIRL

Slow and Solemn

Oh! She's a bad girl, She's a wick-ed girl, My!_____ Oh my!_____ From ale-house to jail-house and all a-long the way, She took a bot-tle of rye, She once met her lov-er, be-gan a quar-rel-ing, Shot him through the core._____ Now she has to die on the gal-lows high, She won't be wick-ed an-y-more._____

BANKS OF THE OHIO

BARBARA ELLEN

Slowly

1. All in the mer - ry month of _____ May, When the green buds they _____ were swell - in', Young _____ Wil - liam Green on his death bed _____ lay, For the
(2. 'Twas in an - oth - er month of _____ May, When the green green buds they _____ were swell - in', Young _____ Wil - liam came o'er a storm - swept _____ bay, And he
(3. And now a - gain 'twas the month of May, When he green had sad news for _____ tell - in', Young _____ Wil - liam Green, on his death bed _____ lay, And he

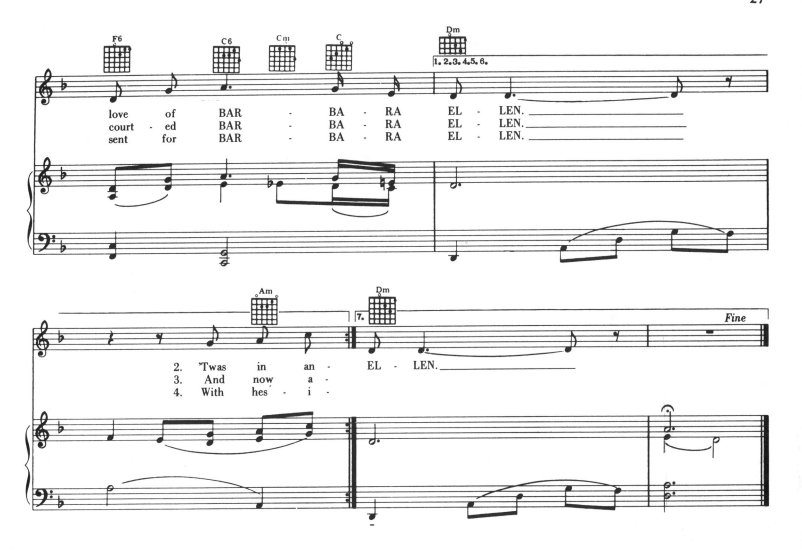

love of BAR - BA - RA EL - LEN.	
court - ed BAR - BA - RA EL - LEN.	
sent for BAR - BA - RA EL - LEN.	

2. 'Twas in an - EL - LEN.
3. And now a -
4. With hes - i -

Fine

4. With hesitation, she came to him,
   She heard the death bell knellin',
   And ev'ry stroke did seem to say:
   You're a mean one, Barbara Ellen.

5. Oh, love, he said, stay beside my bed,
   For my death is on me dwellin',
   And she answered him: Even after you're dead,
   You shan't have Barbara Ellen.

6. His tree of life would be down in the night,
   For trees are meant for fellin',
   Young William Green pleaded: Hold me tight,
   For I love thee, Barbara Ellen.

7. 'Twas not until he passed away,
   'Midst flowers sweet for smellin',
   She realized as she started to pray,
   That she loved him, Barbara Ellen.

BATTLE HYMN OF THE REPUBLIC

1. Mine eyes have seen the glo-ry of the com-ing of the Lord, He is
2. I have seen him in the watch-fires of a hun-dred circ-ling camps, They have
3. I have read a fie-ry gos-pel writ in bur-nish'd rows of steel, "As ye
4. He has sound-ed forth the trum-pet that shall nev-er call re-treat, He is

tramp-ling out the vin-tage where the grapes of wrath are stored, He hath
build-ed him an al-tar in the eve-ning dews and damps, I have
deal with my con-tempt-ers, so with you my grace shall deal", Let the
sift-ing out the hearts of men be-fore his judg-ment seat. O be

loos'd the fate-ful light-ning of his ter-ri-ble, swift sword, His
read his right-eous sen-tence by the dim and flar-ing lamps, His
he-ro born of wo-man crush the ser-pent with his heel, Since
swift, my soul, to an-swer Him, be ju-bil-ant my feet, Our

BEAUTIFUL BROWN EYES

Willie, my darlin', I love you, _____ I love you with all of my heart. _____ Tomorrow we might have been married, _____ But ramblin' has kept us a-

BIG ROCK CANDY MOUNTAIN

Oh, the buzz-in' of the bees and the cig-a-rette trees, The so-da wa-ter foun-tain; Where the lem-on-ade springs and the blue-bird sings On that BIG ROCK CAN-DY MOUN-TAIN. ___ MOUN-TAIN. ___

1. On a sum-mer's day in the month of May, A bur-ly bum came a-hik-in', Down a shad-y lane near the sug-ar cane, He was look-in' for his lik-in'. As he strolled a-long, he sang a song of the

BILLY BOY

CARELESS LOVE

BLUE TAIL FLY

3. The pony jump, he run, he pitch,
   He threw my master in the ditch.
   My master died and who'll deny,
   The blame was on the blue-tail fly.

4. Ole massa's dead and gone to rest,
   They say it happened for the best,
   I won't forget until I die
   Ole massa and the blue-tail fly.

5. A skeeter bites right through your clothes,
   A hornet strikes you on the nose,
   The bees may get you passing by,
   But oh much worse, the blue-tail fly.

CARRY ME BACK TO OLD VIRGINNY

Long by the old dis - mal swamp have I wan-dered, There's where this old dar - key's

life will pass a - way. Mas - sa and Mis- sus have __ gone long be - fore me,

Soon we will meet on that bright and gold - en shore, There we'll be hap - py and

free from all sor - row. There's where we'll meet and we'll __ nev - er part no more.

D.S. %

D.S. al Fine

CHILLY WINDS

Slowly

1. I'm head-in' where those Chil-ly Winds don't blow, ___ my sweet ba - by, I'm

head-in' where those Chil-ly Winds don't blow, _____ When I'm

gone to my long lone-some home. _____ I'm

2. I'm goin' where the cold won't chill my bones, my sweet baby.
I'm goin' where the cold won't chill my bones.
When I'm gone to my long lonesome home.

3. I'm goin' where the folks all know me well, my sweet baby.
I'm goin' where the folks all know me well, my sweet baby.
When I'm gone to my long lonesome home.

4. Now, who will be your honey when I'm gone, my sweet baby.
Now, who will be your honey when I'm gone, my sweet baby.
When I'm gone to my long lonesome home.

CINDY

COPPER KETTLE

CORRINA, CORRINA

CRIPPLE CREEK

Moderato

I got a gal at the head of the creek
Girls on the Crip-ple Creek 'bout half grown
Crip-ple Creek's wide and Crip-ple Creek's deep

go up to see her 'bout the mid-dle of the week.
jump on a boy like a dog on a bone.
I'll wade old Crip-ple Creek a - fore I sleep.

Kiss her on the mouth just as sweet as an-y wine
Roll my britch-es up to my knees I'll
Roads are rock-y and the hill - side's mud-dy and

THE CRUEL WAR

The cruel war is rag - ing, John - ny has to fight. I want to be with him. From morn - ing till night.

VERSION I (continued)

2. Oh Johnny, dear Johnny,
   Morning, noon and night,
   I think of you marching,
   Left, right, left and right.

3. I know you're so gentle,
   When you hold me tight,
   Oh how will they make you -
   Get out there and fight?

4. Go speak to your sergeant,
   And say you want "out",
   Just say you're allergic
   To this kind of bout.

5. Oh Johnny, dear Johnny,
   Yes, I know you're brave,
   But oh! how I miss you,
   It's your love I crave.

6. Oh why did the army -
   Take you from my side,
   To go into battle,
   Away from your bride?

VERSION II (Optional)

1. The cruel war is raging,
   Johnny has to fight,
   I want to be with him,
   From morning till night.

2. I'm counting the minutes,
   The hours and the days,
   Oh Lord, stop the cruel war,
   For this my heart prays.

3. I made my decision,
   I will join up too,
   Oh Johnny, dear Johnny,
   I'll soon be with you.

4. We women are fighters,
   We can help you win,
   Oh Johnny, I'm hoping -
   That they'll take me in.

5. The cruel war is raging,
   Johnny has to fight,
   And I'll be there with him,
   From morning till night.

DARLIN' COREY

DELIA'S GONE (ONE MORE ROUND)

3. He wanted to marry
But she preferred to be loose,
She did not want a goose to cook
And so he cooked her goose.
Delia gone, one more round,
Delia gone! (Chorus)

4. So Tony was locked up,
The judge refused to set bail,
For such a crime, he should do time,
Say, 99 years in jail.
Delia gone, one more round,
Delia gone! (Chorus)

5. Then Tony said "Thank You",
"Your honor treated me fine."
He knew the judge could well have said:
Nine hundred ninety - nine.
Delia gone, one more round,
Delia gone! (Chorus)

DOWN IN THE VALLEY

Moderately bright

1. DOWN IN THE VAL -
2. Give my heart ease,
3. Write me a let -
4. This gloom - y pris

LEY, the val - ley so low, ____
love, oh give my heart ease, ____
ter with just a few lines, ____
on is far from you, dear, ____

Hang your head o - ver, Hear the wind
Think of me, dar - ling, oh give my heart
An - swer me, dar - ling, and say you'll be
But not for ev - er I'm out in a

blow, ____ Hear the wind blow,
ease. ____ Write me a let -
mine. ____ Ros - es love sun -
year. ____ I make this prom

THE ERIE CANAL

FOLLOW THE DRINKING GOURD

FRANKIE AND JOHNNY

1. FRANK - IE AND JOHN - NY were lov - ers,
2. FRANK - IE AND JOHN - NY went walk - ing,
3. John - ny said, "I've _____ got to leave now,

Said they were real - ly in love; Now,
John - ny had on _____ a new suit; That
But I won't be _____ ver - y long; Don't

Frank - ie was true _____ to her John - ny, True as
Frank - ie had bought _____ with a "C - note", 'Cause it
sit up and wait _____ for me, hon - ey, Don't you

4. Frankie went down to the hotel,
   Looked in the window so high,
   There she saw her lovin' Johnny -
   Making love to Nellie Bly,
   He was her man but he done her wrong.

5. Johnny saw Frankie a-comin',
   Down the back stairs he did scoot,
   Frankie, she took out her pistol,
   Oh that lady sure could shoot!
   He was her man but he done her wrong.

6. Frankie, she went to the big chair,
   Calm as a lady could be,
   Turning her eyes up, she whisper'd -
   Lord, I'm coming up to Thee,
   He was my man, but he done me wrong.

GIVE ME THAT OLD TIME RELIGION

GOOBER PEAS

GO TELL IT ON THE MOUNTAIN

3. And lo! When they had heard it,
   They all bowed down to pray,
   Then travel'd on together,
   To where the Baby lay. (Chorus)

4. When I was just a learner,
   I sought by night and day,
   To have the Good Lord help me,
   To guide me on my way. (Chorus)

5. I too am like a shepherd,
   My flock of days to guard,
   Each day finds time for praying,
   From this I won't retard. (Chorus)

HOUSE OF THE RISING SUN

I GAVE MY LOVE A CHERRY

IT'S HARD, AIN'T IT HARD?

1. IT'S HARD, AIN'T IT HARD, ain't it hard? ____ To give love that
2. (The) first time I saw you, I knew ____ There's man-y a-
3. (You) like ev-'ry-one ex-cept me, ____ And yet I'm the

won't come back to you. ____ IT'S HARD, AIN'T IT HARD, ain't it
run-nin' af-ter you. ____ IT'S HARD, AIN'T IT HARD, ain't it
one whose love is true, ____ IT'S HARD, AIN'T IT HARD, ain't it

real, real hard, To love you, my love, the way I do. ____ 2. The
real, real hard, To love you, my love, the way I do. ____ 3. You
real, real hard, To love you, my love, the way I do. ____

I'M A MAN OF CONSTANT SORROW

4. I'm a man of constant sorrow,
   A stranger in every town,
   Friends I have none to give me comfort,
   While I go roaming 'round.

5. I'm a man of constant sorrow,
   My face you may see no more,
   One thing I know I can be sure of,
   We'll meet on one same shore.

6. I'm a man of constant sorrow,
   I've seen trouble all my days,
   I left my home in old Kentucky,
   Where I was born and raised.

I NEVER WILL MARRY

Slow waltz tempo

mf

mp

1. Oh I nev - er will mar - ry, I will
2. Oh I nev - er will mar - ry, I will

be no man's wife, I in - tend to be
keep my - self free, Love is sel - dom the

sin - gle for the rest _____ of my life. Oh I
sweet thing that it's cracked _____ up to be, So I

3. Oh I never will marry,
   No, I won't tie the knot,
   'Cause I'm really contented -
   With the freedom I've got.
   No, I never will marry,
   If I lie, strike me dead,
   No! I never will marry,
   Not at least till I'm wed.

4. Oh I never will marry,
   I'll just stay on the shelf
   I will care for nobody,
   I'll just care about myself.
   Oh I never will marry,
   Marriage fills me with dread,
   So I never will marry,
   Not at least till I'm wed.

5. Oh I never will marry,
   I will be no man's wife,
   I intend to stay single -
   For the rest of my life.
   Oh I never will marry,
   I will share no man's bed,
   No! I never will marry,
   Not at least till I'm wed.

I WISH I WAS SINGLE AGAIN

MATILDA

JESSE JAMES

1. JES - SE JAMES was a lad who ___ killed man - y a man, Once he
2. JES - SE JAMES was a friend, and he helped ev - 'ry - one out, With the
3. JES - SE JAMES took a name, "Jim - my How - ard", ___ and flew to a

robbed the Glen - dale ___ train. He would steal from the rich, he would
loot he stole from the bank. When a robb - 'ry oc - curred, No ___
town where he was - n't known. But his friend Rob - ert Ford, neith - er

give to the poor, Had a hand and a heart ___ and a
one had a doubt, It was he and his dear ___ broth - er
faith - ful nor true, Turned a - gainst him and caught ___ him a

JOHN HARDY

1. JOHN HAR - DY was a man, yes a hard hit - tin'
2. JOHN HAR - DY was a man, you could nev - er de -

man, His pis - tol was his pal night and
ceive, He held a pair of a - ces and one

day. _____ He shot and he killed and as
day. _____ Bill Jones had three kings, one was

81

3. John Hardy might have lived as a free man today,
   Except for one mistake that he made,
   He went for to see if his fam'ly was O.K.,
   And the law was a-waitin' out in the shade, Oh Lord!
   And the law was a law that had to be paid.

4. John Hardy called himself just a fair-fightin' man,
   He said he had good reason to kill.
   He once ripped an arm from saloonkeeper, Dan,
   'Cause he sold watered whiskey out of a still, Oh Lord!
   Hardy bought watered whiskey out of a still.

5. John Hardy spoke these words with a noose 'round his neck,
   "My absence won't make anyone grieve.
   If this be the price, guess I'll have to pay the check,
   But I lost 'cause a card was up in his sleeve, Oh Lord!
   And John Hardy, he 'lows no card in a sleeve."

JOHN HENRY

4. John Henry took a heavy hammer,
   And, beside the steam drill he did stand.
   He was faster than the drill, but oh! alas!
   He died with the hammer in his hand, O Lord!
   Died with the hammer in his hand.

5. So they took John Henry to the graveyard,
   And they laid him down into the sand,
   And when any locomotive passed the grave,
   'Tis said the engineer would look and say:
   There lies a steel-drivin' man.

6. John Henry, he's an inspiration,
   To the men whose hands are born for toil,
   Even in this day and age of automation,
   Digging coal, drilling for the precious oil,
   Nothing beats a hammer-hitting man.

JOHN RILEY

Her cheeks were like a lil - y fair.

(See additional lyrics) more.

2. Then I went up and I spoke with caution,
   Would'st like to be a sailor's wife?
   Oh no, oh no, she quickly answered,
   I wish to live the single life.

3. Said I "Fair maid, why are you so different -
   From all the rest of woman-kind?
   You are so fair, so completely lovely,
   To marry you, I am inclined."

4. Said she "Kind sir, I was set to marry,
   Some two or three long years ago,
   'Twas to a man whom they call John Riley,
   Who was the cause of all my woe."

5. "I'll not leave off thinking of John Riley,
   Nor go with you as you implore,
   My heart is his and I can't forsake him,
   Although his face I'll see no more.

6. 'Twas then I saw that her love was constant,
   The kiss I gave was full and free.
   "My looks have changed, but I'm still John Riley,
   I came back rich - to marry thee."

JUST A CLOSER WALK WITH THEE

KUM BA YAH

LA BAMBA

MALAGUEÑA SALEROSA

MAMA DON'T 'LOW

1. MA - MA DON'T 'LOW no danc - ing par - ties 'round here, _____ Oh no! My MA - MA DON'T 'LOW no danc - ing par - ties 'round here. _____ Well,

2. MA - MA DON'T 'LOW no par - lor neck - in' 'round here, _____ Oh no! My MA - MA DON'T 'LOW no par - lor neck - in' 'round here. _____ Well,

3. Mama don't 'low no drums a-drummin' 'round here,
   No banjos, guitars a-strummin' 'round here,
   Well she's not here to rave and shout,
   And the Joneses living next door went out,
   Mama don't 'low no drums a-drummin' 'round here.

4. Mama don't 'low no loud mouth talkin' 'round here,
   Mama don't 'low no loud mouth talkin' 'round here,
   Well, I don't care what mama don't 'low,
   Gonna shoot my mouth off anyhow.
   Mama don't 'low no loud mouth talkin' 'round here.

5. Mama don't 'low no nuthin' going on here,
   Mama don't 'low no nuthin' going on here,
   Well, I don't see why my mama don't 'low,
   She was once as young as we are now,
   Mama don't 'low no nuthin' going on here.

MICHAEL

MIDNIGHT SPECIAL

2. Well if you're ever in Houston,
   You'd better walk on by
   Oh, you'd better not gamble, boy
   I say you'd better not fight.
   Well now, the sheriff, he'll grab you
   And his boys will pull you down
   And then before you know it
   You're penitentiary-bound.
        (To Chorus) A-let the Midnight Special etc.

3. Here comes Miss Lucy
   How in the world do you know?
   I know by her apron
   And by the dress she wore.
   An umbrella on her shoulder
   A piece of paper in her hand
   She gonna see the sheriff
   To try to free her man.
        (To Chorus) A-let the Midnight Special etc.

MOUNTAIN DEW

Verse:

1. I know a place 'bout a mile down the road, Where you
2. High on a hill, there's a se - clud - ed still, And it's
3. My broth - er, Paul, he is tin - y and small, And he
4. Miss Jane Mac - Hume tried a brand - new per - fume, It had

lay down a dol - lar or two. _____ If you
run by a hard work - ing crew. _____ You can
meas - ures a - bout four foot two, _____ But he
oh such a sweet smell - ing pu. _____ Was the

hush up your mug, they will slip you a jug of that
tell ve - ry well, as you snif - fle a smell, it's that
thinks he's a gi'nt when they give him a pint of that
la - dy sur - prised when it was a - na - lyzed As that

good OLD MOUN - TAIN DEW. _____ They
good OLD MOUN - TAIN DEW. _____ They
good OLD MOUN - TAIN DEW. _____ They
good OLD MOUN - TAIN DEW. _____

1.2.3.   4.

MULE SKINNER BLUES

MOCKINGBIRD (HUSH, LITTLE BABY)

NINE POUND HAMMER

NOBODY KNOWS THE TROUBLE I'VE SEEN

OLD BLUE

1. I had an old dog, _____ and his name was Blue, _____
(2. The 'pos-sum he) chased, _____ up a 'sim-mon tree, _____

_____ And I betch-a five dol-lars he's a good dog, too, _____ Oh there's ver-y
_____ Oh there nev-er was a pos-sum hound as good as he. ____ Oh there's ver-y

few _____ dogs like my OLD BLUE. _____
few _____ dogs like my OLD BLUE. _____

3. I had an old dog, and his name was Blue,
   But he died and left me like he had to do,
   I said "Go on, Blue,
   I'm a-comin' too."

4. In Heaven some day, first thing I'll do,
   Gonna grab my horn and blow for Old Dog Blue
   I'll say "Come on, Blue,
   Fin'lly got here too."

5. I dug him a grave, and I put him down,
   And I carved a wooden marker which I bought in town,
   And I said "Old Blue,
   I'm a-comin' too."

OLD JOE CLARK

Moderato, not too fast

Old Joe Clark, the preach-er's son, preached all o-ver the
used to live on a moun-tain top but now I live in
When I was a lit-tle girl I used to play with

plain, The on-ly text he ev-er used was
town I'm board-ing at the big ho-tel
toys Now I am a big-ger girl I

"High, low, jack and the game."
court-ing Bet-sy Brown.
rath-er play with boys.

REFRAIN

Round and a-round, Old Joe Clark,

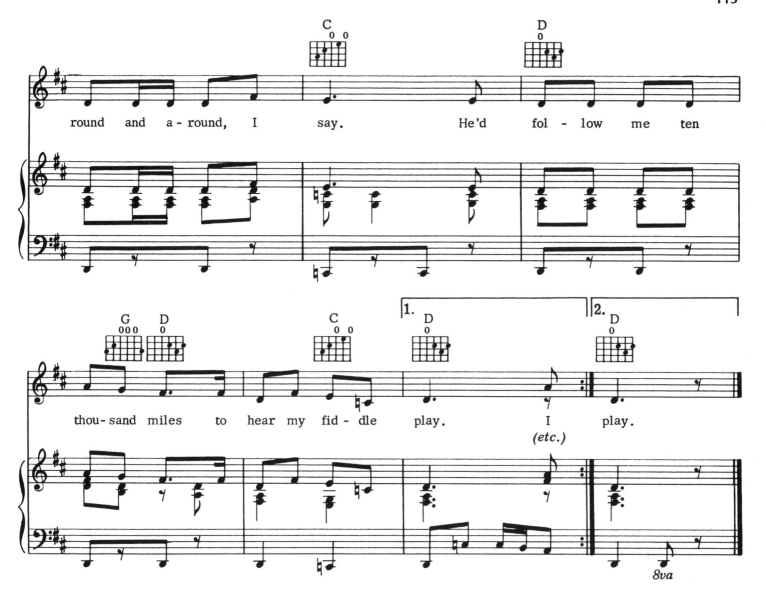

round and a-round, I say. He'd fol-low me ten thou-sand miles to hear my fid-dle play. I play. *(etc.)*

When I was a little boy,
I used to want a knife;
Now I am a bigger boy,
I only want a wife.

Wish I was a sugar tree,
Standin' in the middle of some town;
Ev'ry time a pretty girl passed,
I'd shake some sugar down.

Old Joe had a yellow cat,
She would not sing or pray;
She stuck her head in a buttermilk jar
And washed her sins away.

I wish I had a sweetheart;
I'd set her on the shelf,
And ev'ry time she'd smile at me
I'd get up there myself.

OLD PAINT

1. I   ride   an OLD   PAINT,   I   lead   old
2. Old   Biff   Jones   had two   daugh - ters   and a
3. When   I   die,   take my   sad - dle   from the

Dan,   I'm a - going   to Mon -   tan'   for to   throw   the   hool - i -
song;   One   went to   Den - ver,   the   oth -   er   went
wall;   Lead   out my   po - ny, lead him   out   of   his

han; They feed in the cool-ie, they wa- ter in the
wrong; His wife, she died in a pool___ room___
stall; Tie my bones to the sad-dle, turn his face to-ward the

draw, Their tails are all mat-ted, their backs are all raw.
fight, But still he keeps on sing-in' from morn-ing to night.
west And we'll ride the prai- rie that we love the best.

Chorus

Ride a- round, lit-tle dog-ie, Ride a- round 'em slow;___ The

fir- ey and the snuf-fy Are a- rar- in' to go. go.

RAILROAD BILL

1. Rail-road Bill, Rail-road Bill, Hates to work and I guess he nev-er will.
2. Sit - tin' still on a hill, Man - y a train pass-es

Rail-road Bill. 1.Once he got him-self a B. B. gun, When he saw the noon ex-

press train run, Took a shot and hit the en - gi - neer, Land-ed in the clink for a

2. Ev'ryone is wond'ring how he lives,
   Never takes a penny, never gives.
   Even heard a rumor going 'round,
   That he robbed a bank in a nearby town.

   Railroad Bill, Railroad Bill,
   Hates to work and I guess he never will.
   Sittin' still - on a hill,
   Many a train passes Railroad Bill.

3. Would you like employment? Someone
      said.
   He replied: I'd rather see me dead.
   Wasn't born to be a working guy,
   Let me sit and watch how the trains
      go by.

   Railroad Bill, Railroad Bill,
   Hates to work and I guess he never will.
   Sittin' still - on a hill,
   Many a train passes Railroad Bill.

ROCK-A MY SOUL

ROCK ISLAND LINE

fly - in', Buy your tick - et at the sta - tion on the ROCK IS - LAND

LINE. 1. I LINE. know I'm right when I say it's

fine, It's real - ly great to ride on the ROCK IS - LAND LINE!

2. Now this here train has but one design,
   To get you where you're going,
   The Rock Island Line! (Chorus)

3. And man, oh man! It's a place divine,
   For kissing in the tunnels
   The Rock Island Line! (Chorus)

4. Its destination ain't really mine,
   But anyhow, I'll take it,
   The Rock Island Line! (Chorus)

SCARBOROUGH FAIR

Slowly, with feeling

Are you go - ing to Scar - bor - ough
Tell her to make me a cam - bric

Fair? Pars - ley, sage, _____ rose -
shirt, Pars - ley, sage, _____ rose -

ma - ry and thyme; Re - mem - ber
ma - ry and thyme; With - out any

124

SALTY DOG

SEE SEE RIDER

Moderately Bright

Oh, See,   See See Rid - er,   Girl, See
I'm go-in',   go-in' a-way, ba - by,   And I won't be

What You've Done,_   Woa _____   See See Rid -
back 'til Fall,____   Yes____ I'm go - in',   go-in' a - way,

er,   See   What You've Done _ now,
ba - by,   And I won't be   back 'til Fall, ___

You've gone a - way and left ____ me, girl ____ now, ____
Gon-na find me a good look-in' wo-man, no, no, ____ no, ____

and now the blues has come.
I won't be back at

Now, See See Rid - er, I

love you, yes, I do, ____ And there is-n't one thing, dar - lin', I

would not do for you. __ You know why I want you, See, __ See, I

SINGLE GIRL

3. When I was single, I ate biscuit pie.
   Now I am married, eat cornbread or die. [*Refrain*]

4. Two little babies all for to retain.
   Neither one able to help me one grain. [*Refrain*]

5. One crying, "Mama, I want a piece of bread."
   One crying, "Mama, I want to go to bed." [*Refrain*]

6. Wash them and dress them and put them to bed,
   Before your man curses them and wishes you were dead. [*Refrain*]

SHADY GROVE

Fast Dance

Peach - es in the sum - mer - time, Ap - ples in the fall, If

I can't get the girl I love, Won't have none at all.

Chorus:

Shad - y grove, my true love, Shad - y grove, I know

Shad - y grove, my true love, I'm bound for the Shad - y grove.

2. Once I was a little boy,
   Playin' in the sand,
   Now I am a great big boy,
   I think myself a man.
   Chorus

3. When I was a little boy,
   I wanted a whittlin' knife;
   Now I am a great big boy,
   An' I want a little wife.
   Chorus

4. Wish I had a banjo string,
   Made of golden twine,
   And every tune I'd pick on it—
   Is "I wish that girl were mine".
   Chorus

6. Ev'ry night when I go home,
   My wife, I try to please her,
   The more I try, the worse she gets,
   Damned if I don't leave her.
   Chorus

7. Fly around, my blue-eyed girl,
   Fly around, my daisy,
   Fly around, my blue-eyed girl,
   Nearly drive me crazy.
   Chorus

8. The very next time I go that road
   And it don't look so dark and grazy,
   The very next time I come that road,
   I'll stop and see my daisy.
   Chorus

SHENANDOAH

Moderately with feeling

mf

1. Oh SHEN - AN - DOAH, I long to
2. Oh SHEN - AN - DOAH, I love to your

mf

hear you, A - way you roll - ing
daught - er, A - way you roll - ing

riv - er, _____ Oh SHEN - AN - DOAH, _____ I long to
riv - er, _____ Oh SHEN - AN - DOAH, _____ I love your

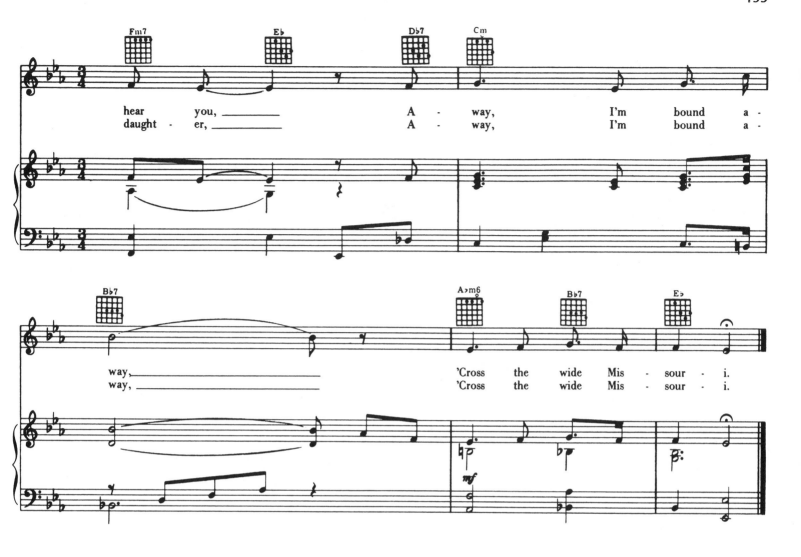

3. 'Tis seven long years since last I saw you,
   Away, you rolling river,
   'Tis seven long years since last I saw you,
   Away, I'm bound away,
   'Cross the wide Missouri.

4. Oh Shenandoah, I love your daughter,
   Away, you rolling river,
   Oh Shenandoah, I'll come to claim her,
   Away, I'm bound away,
   'Cross the wide Missouri.

5. In all these years, whene'er I saw her,
   We have kept our love a secret,
   Oh! Shenandoah, I do adore her,
   Away, I'm bound away,
   'Cross the wide Missouri.

6. Oh Shenandoah, she's bound to leave you,
   Away, you rolling river,
   Oh Shenandoah, I'll not deceive you,
   Away, I'm bound away,
   'Cross the wide Missouri.

SILKIE

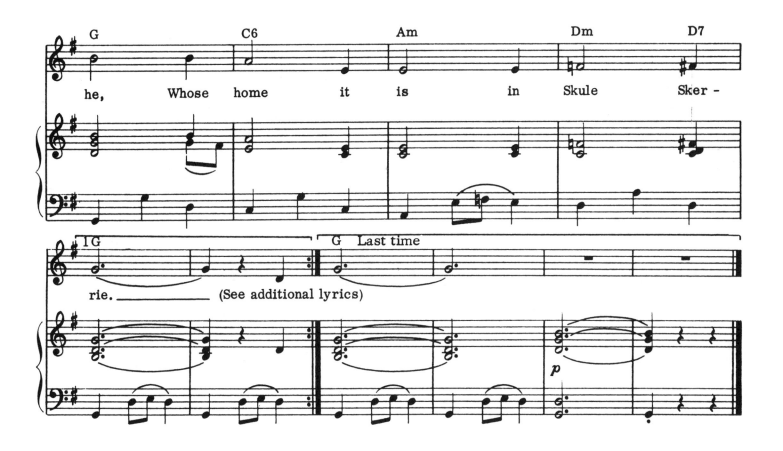

rie. _____ (See additional lyrics)

2. When he be man, he takes a wife,
   When he be beast, he takes her life.
   Ladies, beware of him who be -
   A silkie come from Skule Skerrie.

3. His love they willingly accept,
   But after they have loved and slept,
   Who is the monster that they see?
   'Tis "Silkie" come from Skule Skerrie.

4. A maiden from the Orkney Isles,
   A target for his charm, his smiles,
   Eager for love, no fool was she,
   She knew the secret of Skule Skerrie.

5. And so, while Silkie kissed the lass,
   She rubbed his neck with Orkney grass,
   This had the magic power, you see -
   To slay the beast from Skule Skerrie.

THE SILVER DAGGER

1. Sing no love songs, You'll wake my moth - er, She's sleep - ing here, Right by my side,
2. You're the wrong one, So says my moth - er, I ought to wed a man of wealth.
3. Go my lov - er, Go find a maid - en, My dear sweet moth'r must be o - beyed.

SIXTEEN TONS

SLOOP JOHN B

STEWBALL

4. Supposing he stumbles,
He might even fall,
And he'll still be a winner,
That's my noble Stewball.

5. Stewball was a good horse,
He held a high head,
And the mane on his foretop
Was as fine as silk thread.

6. I rode him in England
I rode him in Spain,
He was never a loser,
And I always did gain.

ST. JAMES INFIRMARY

THE STREETS OF LAREDO

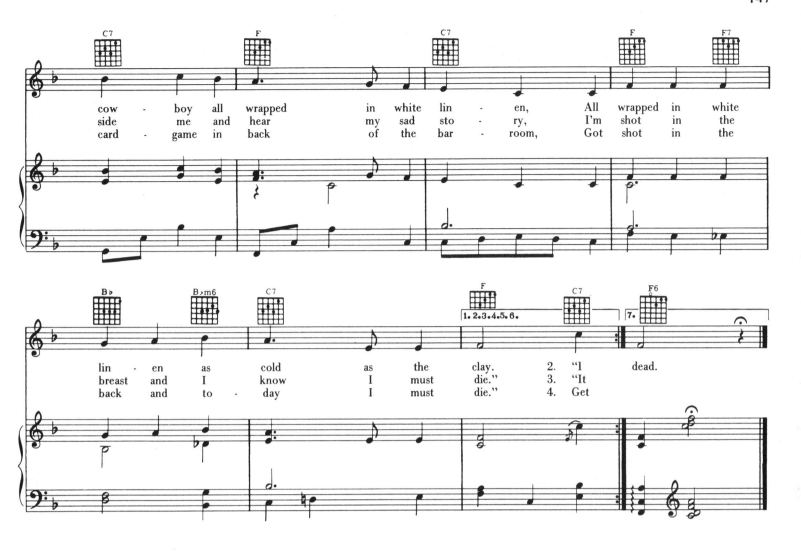

4. Get six of my buddies to carry my coffin,
   And six pretty maidens to sing a sad song,
   Take me to the valley and lay the sod o'er me,
   For I'm a young cowboy who played the game wrong."

5. "Oh, beat the drum slowly and play the fife lowly,
   And play the dead march as they carry my pall.
   Put bunches of roses all over my coffin,
   The roses will deaden the clods as they fall."

6. "Go gather around you a crowd of young cowboys,
   And tell them the story of this my sad fate.
   Tell one and the other before they go further,
   To stop their wild roving before it's too late."

7. "Go fetch me a cup, just a cup of cold water,
   To cool my parched lips," the cowboy then said.
   Before I returned, his brave spirit had left him,
   And, gone to his maker, the cowboy was dead.

TEN THOUSAND MILES

THIS LITTLE LIGHT OF MINE

WABASH CANNON BALL

1. From the great At - lan - tic O - cean to the wide Pa - cif - ic's shore, From the ones we leave be-
2. Lis - ten to the rhyth - mic jin - gle and the rum - ble and the roar, As she glides a - long the
3. She was com - ing from At - lan - ta on a cold De - cem - ber day. As she rolled in - to the

hind us to the ones we see once more. She's might - y tall and hand - some, and
wood - lands thro' the hills and by the shore. You hear the might - y en - gine, and
sta - tion, I could hear a wom - an say: He's might - y big and hand - some, and

quite well known by all, How we love the choo choo of the WA - BASH CAN - NON-
pray that it won't stall, While we safe - ly trav - el on the WA - BASH CAN - NON-
sure did make me fall," "He's a - com - ing tow'rd me on the WA - BASH CAN - NON-

THE WAYFARIN' STRANGER

155

WILDWOOD FLOWER

Lively

1. I'll en- twine and I'll min- gle my ra- ven black
2. Oh he prom- ised to love me, he called me "his
3. But I'll dance and I'll sing, And my heart will be

hair, With the ro- ses so red and the li- lies so fair, And my
flow'r", He said I was the blos- som to cheer ev- 'ry hour. But I
gay, No more tears, no more sighs, No more weep- ing a- way. I'll be

eyes will out- shine e- ven stars in the blue, Said I know- ing
woke from my dream, And my i- dol was clay, This wild- flow- er
'round when I see him Re- gret this dark hour, When he threw a-

not that my love was un- true. _____ (Oh he)
weeps thru the night, thru the day. _____ (But I'll)
way this poor frail WILD- WOOD FLOW'R. _____ FLOW'R. _____

A WORRIED MAN

WHISTLING GYPSY ROVER

Moderately

Verse

1. The gyp-sy ro-ver come o-ver the hill, Bound through the val-ley so sha - dy; He
2. left her fa-ther's ___ cas-tle ___ gate, She left her own true ___ lov - er; She
3. fa-ther sad-dled his fast-est ___ steed, Roamed the ___ val-ley all o - ver; ___
4. came at last to a man-sion ___ fine, Down by the ri-ver ___ Clayde; ___ And
5. He's no gyp-sy my fa--ther, said she, My lord of free-lands all o - ver; And

whist-led and he sang till the green woods rang, And he won the heart of a · la - dy. ___
left ___ her ___ ser-vants and her es - tate, To fol-low the gyp-sy ___ ro - ver. ___
Sought ___ his ___ daugh-ter at great ___ speed, And the WHIST-LING GYP - SY ___ RO - VER. ___
there ___ was ___ mu-sic and there was wine, For the gyp-sy and his ___ la - dy. ___
I ___ will ___ stay till my dy-ing day, With my WHIST-LING GYP - SY ___ RO - VER. ___

Chorus

Ah - di - do, ah - di di - da - day, Ah - di - do, ah - di -

day - dee; He whist - led and he sang till the green woods rang. And

he won the heart of a la dy.

To Verse

2. She
3. Her
4. He
5. ___

Last Time

dy. And he won the heart of a la dy.

THIS TRAIN

Moderately, in two

1. THIS TRAIN is bound for glo - ry, THIS TRAIN. _____ THIS TRAIN is
2. THIS TRAIN don't car - ry no gam - blers, THIS TRAIN. _____ THIS TRAIN is don't
3. THIS TRAIN don't car - ry no li - ars, THIS TRAIN. _____ THIS TRAIN don't

bound for glo - ry, THIS TRAIN. _____ THIS TRAIN is bound for glo - ry,
car - ry no gam - blers, THIS TRAIN. _____ THIS TRAIN don't car - ry no gam - blers, no
car - ry no li - ars, THIS TRAIN. _____ THIS TRAIN don't car - ry no li - ars, the

don't ride noth-in' but the right-eous and the ho - ly,
hyp - o - crites, no mid - night ramb - lers, } THIS TRAIN is bound for glo - ry, THIS TRAIN. _____
truth is what the Lord de - sires,

THIS TRAIN. _____ THIS TRAIN. _____ THIS TRAIN. _____